The Windigo Chronicles

David Groulx

BookLand press

Published by BookLand Press
15 Allstate Parkway, Suite 600
Markham, Ontario L3R 5B4
www.booklandpress.com

Printed in Canada

Front cover image © Adrenalinapura

Library and Archives Canada Cataloguing in Publication

Groulx, David A., 1969-, author
The windigo chronicles / David Groulx.

(Canadian Aboriginal voices series)
Poems.
Issued in print and electronic formats.
ISBN 978-1-77231-038-2 (paperback).--ISBN 978-1-77231-039-9 (epub).--ISBN 978-1-77231-040-5 (pdf)

I. Title. II. Series: Canadian Aboriginal voices

PS8563.R76W56 2016 C811'.54 C2016-904768-7
C2016-904769-5

Canada Council for the Arts Conseil des arts du Canada

ONTARIO ARTS COUNCIL
CONSEIL DES ARTS DE L'ONTARIO
an Ontario government agency
un organisme du gouvernement de l'Ontario

We acknowledge the support of the Canada Council for the Arts, which last year invested $153 million to bring the arts to Canadians throughout the country. We acknowledge the support of the Ontario Arts Council (OAC), an agency of the Government of Ontario. We acknowledge the financial support of the Ontario Media Development Corporation for our publishing activities.

Dedicated to the memory
of my friend
Renate Eigenbrod

First we ate our dogs
because they understood the true meaning of devotion
and then we ate our horses
because the moose and deer could no longer be found
and then we ate the grass
because at that time the land was still ours

Windigo lived in a stone lodge
and dreamed of eating Indians
said their feet tasted best of all the flesh
and then asked for forgiveness
his icy heart hidden beneath
the deep wind from the north

It was then
just after the last creation
that Jiibayaabooz[1] challenged the Great North Wind
he hid in the deep snow and said
"I am not afraid of you Great North Wind
you came by the frozen water
I know where you came from
I will cut you to pieces brother"
and snow spilled over snow

Jiibayaabooz sang
Jiisakiwin[2]
and the spirit of Mikinaak[3]
"Only with you, great and mighty
axe can you split the Great North Wind
furious, even after death
dread dear Hare
I have flown the world and
the Great North Wind cannot be found
he is coming
he is on his way
you must prepare
fury you have not known
I must go
the Anishnabeg[4] call me"

The factor brought with him
the faces of four horses
the Great North Wind had never seen
a white man before
Jiibayaabooz
stood on his hind feet
and saw the man
curled up above the trees

Hare removed some boughs
and dug a hole beneath
for here was where he kept
his great axe
the very one he used to kill
some giants long ago

First Hare took his
axe and killed a mooz[5] because he was hungry
chopped off the head and adorned it
in beads and shells
singing softly
Megwetch, Chi Megwetch[6]
for sustaining our lives
he blew tobacco smoke to mooz injichaag[7]
ate some of it
the rest he shared
with some Indians he met
then he waited for the
bones above the trees

Hare fell asleep and dreamed that
meat fell from the sky
Indians became otters
and his children became young moose
but Hare would not eat

"Great North Wind is coming"
he said to the Indians
"but I have dreamed good dreams
and have not eaten any snow or ice
I will meet her
not my brothers
Nanboozhoo, Maudjee-kawiss or Pukawiss
my great axe
will meet her
that one that kills for a
little while."

Cheeno[8]! Atoosh[9]! Bakaak[10]!
ahhh Windigo
old woman
I have my deerskin cord
to fasten you
to snap your head from your neck

Jiibayaabooz began to build
a pyre near the place
where Animikiig[11]
laid her stone eggs
a high cliff
in the days when
the Beaver people still spoke
before Indians grew tired of war
end of heroes

Hare took out his whetstone
and began to sharpen his axe
this up to ten Indians could not lift
he smoothed out the dents and scrapes
from the days of giants and their herds of great
horned beasts
trampling the earth
he made new it's bite

Now the Great North Wind
turned the land upside down
and shook it
but only Indians
and a few beaver fell out
no Hare
she walked up and down the rivers
causing them to flow backwards
even Mishi ginebeg[12] was afraid

She travelled to the Sweetgrass Hills
looking under the corpses of dead Indians
then onto the Cypress Hills
more corpses
food for Mahigan[13]
who was also starving

Then she sent out Bakaak
who stalked and killed
all the Indians he could find
so many he killed!
so many he slaughtered!
their bones became like snow

Bakaak flew over both sides of the fresh ghettos[14]
and rotting faces[15]
ate the raw flesh
that fell from his bones
that was namebini-giizis[16]
he went strong
howling from the Forks
to the Trois-Rivières
all the way to the French forts
even the birch bark canoes
cowered beneath the ugly blow

The loup-garou[17] gored
all the Indians' dogs
he spread out all the entrails
in a circle
and only ate the toughest livers
"Wemitigoozh[18] come out of
your meagre abode!"

He stood outside the fort
and taunted
"Give me good measure!
lo poore moi[19]
your madness and crucifix
my dogs are
all dead and no longer faithful
to the lash"

He dragged their lifeless
bodies to the French gates
"I have beaver Frenchman!
the kind you love
winter beaver and
summer beaver too
this four-legged
caretaker of the waters
my brother loves more
than me"

I've come far brother
from the country of
rotting faces
that country that
God gave to Cain[20]
where copper belongs

only to that underwater lynx[21]
whose sadness overwhelmed
the world
drowning beaver and muskrat
causing them to visit that place
where food tastes like ash
and everything is only a shadow of itself
that direction
the last place
the pipe bows too

You do not know this land Wemitigoozh
this land that followed Meegis[22]
the Anishnabeg and Nanaboozho
chased down plenty of mooz and waawaashkeshi[23]
now there is none to be found

Wemitigoozh!
Show me merci[24]
open your gates to moi
a poore loup-garou
I've slaughtered and eaten
my entire family

I've gorged on their flesh and
still I was not full
I began to hunt Indians
because they looked like
young moose calves to me
even the tender rotting faces I ate
and those that are left
will not come to your
house Frenchman!
whose god is your master?
whose god hangs from a tree?

Have mercy on me as he has had on you
I forgive you for your trespass
I've done nothing to be forgiven for
your sky father who does not inhabit this land
this land is holy to us Frenchman
I, the loup-garou, who
made you cedar tea
carried your arses
over my land
through the vast
cornfields of the Wendat[25]
who paddled the great canoes
all the way to the lakehead
made offerings and libations

to the great copper god
under the great sea
piled high your storehouses
with muskrat and deer

Now you turn me away
to the land of the Abenaqui[26]
land of our brothers
who first saw Meegis
who witnessed Mahigan slaughter
Mishi pishu's[27] children
I almost cried myself
Frenchman!
the sun comes down on us
the darkness gathers around us
let me warm myself by your fires
that I may use you kettle
to cook that magical
terrible feast

♦ ♦ ♦

Jiibayaabooz gathered boulders
those grandfathers of old
before the giants passed and their
countless mammoth herds
when the Nadoüessioüak[28] built
their houses in the trees
to escape them and their destruction
he turned to the mountains
and fetched water from the Kitchissippi[29]

Jiiayaabooz piled up a soaring fire
naked in his sweat he invoked
his ancestors to send him a vision
to the keeper of the Makwa[30]
who knows the medicine that restores
the world
to the keeper of the Ma'iingan[31]
who knows the loyalty to family
that caused him to kill
the underwater serpent's children
that act that was done
that starving Nanahboozhoo
might eat

He implored the keeper of Makwa
who gave the Anishnabeg
many strong and good medicines
to the underwater beings he prayed
bowing his pipe and smoking
four times
to the four directions he offered
his pipe of asemaa[32]
he heaped more water
on the grandfathers
and steam rose
that he might visit the spirit world
that he might defeat
the Great North Wind

The keeper of Makwa came to Jiibayaabooz's lodge
coming in from the eastern door
and the fiercest of the underwater
manitous whose name cannot be spoken
but only when the deepest of
ice covers his abode
and those elders began to teach Jiibayaabooz
a song
they began to sing that sacred music
that all the earth might hear
a song as a weapon

a song as a gift
to Jiibayaabooz
the song the bends over
turtle's back

This is how the spirit world
touches this one
song that moves across the universe
and shakes the land
from that time that time
cannot measure
they kept singing
they smudged with a braid of hair
from the earth mother
that all life
and medicine to each
they smudged with sage
that medicine
was given to Anishnabegiikew[33]
to acknowledge woman's power
to give life
they drank cedar tea
to refresh the body
the fourth medicine
to heal the body
they sang until the sun fell into its

silent lodge
and the ancient grandfathers
left and stones consumed

Jiibayaabooz fell exhausted into
a deep sleep
he found himself walking on an old trail
there he came across an old Indian woman
sitting at an darkened fire pit
without fire
she did not speak
nindizhinikaaz[34] Jiibayaabooz
niin nindoonjibaa[35] Waabanong[36]
he pulled some smouldering embers
from his testicles and lit that fire
the old woman said nothing

He spied Bakaak on a dog train
only bones
he was on his way to the nation of the Abenaqui
nearer and nearer
he drew to their dreams
Bakaak called out
Zhaaganaash[37]! I am coming
I am nigh
Nookomis madwe-biibaagi agaaming?[38]
the ice groaning beneath me

I am malice, at my feet are terror
and a ferocious loathing
I am bearing down
Zhaaganaash
over to the country of the Lenni Lenapes[39]
you Zhaaganaash
who squawks like a little bird
in the forest
who claims the coast
for his king across the sea
that water that sustains the Mik'maq
the Abenaqui, the Beothuk
the Wampanoag
they all love this land
the land of our ancestors
who were put here
by Gichi-manidoo[40]
you who wonders
wanders like the wind
around the world like Bakaak
leaving the graves of your ancestors
Zhaaganaash who shudders at
how many Indians are breathing
on the other side of the Apalwahči[41] mountains
near where the great horned snake abides
who makes the earth shake

Here I am
a mere faun
a faun to you Englishman!
look at me
covered in English blankets
I've watched brown men die
and their lives
were no different from yours
where are our brothers the Powhatan?
the Susquehannock?
the Mahican?

I've come here to Lenapehoking[42]
all the way from Stadacona[43]
I've brought many deer hide
Ah yes waawaashkeshi
to trade with my friends
tell me Zhaaganaash
what the hell did you do with all
those damn Indians
and all those damn deer?
did you hide them under a rock?
only a great rock would be able to hide all
those Indians

Have you taken them back to your country?
in your great wiigwaasi-jiimaan[44]
are they in your fort?
huddled near your fires
stirring kettles of sap
to make syrup?

They were here when I was last here
I watched them, baaga'adowe[45]
feasted with them
sweated with them
I am all that is left
outside your palissade[46] with
not even a pot to piss in
boiling the bones of my ancestors
whom we love
and who love us
that marrow of this earth
Zhagaanaash who loves zhooniyaa[47]
more than gimishoomis[48]

What have you done to my Indians?
I am starving like you were in Roanoke
I remembered you
Gaunt bastards of the sea
not even she wanted you

puked you out of the water
here in the land of the dawn people
they too, are now gone
I miss them most
even the meanest of dogs
is a sad beast at the loss
howling in the empty night
they have vanished

What is life?
It is the flash of a firefly in the night
It is the breath of a buffalo in the wintertime
It is the little shadow which runs across
the grass and loses itself in the sunset[49]

Hunted down and slaughtered
not even anyone left to bury
the bodies
to mourn
except my guile, yoke and mania
come now Zhagaanaash
I have travelled so far and so many miles
and I am so hungry
pity me
this poor faun of the forest
I beckon you to let me into

your palisade
a kettle for my feet
oh! my paws oh! hooves
true the Allegheny
to your tiny fart
your small gaol
I who taught you
to plant corn, squash, beans
tomatoes, potatoes, tobacco
give me good measure!
Zhagaanaash
where's your king who claims this land?
I do not see him
I do not even see you
hidden away in your shack
I name these lands
I name this land!
I am bound to it
like a woman to her husband
like a child to his father

The Great North Wind is coming
Englishman
can you hear the howling wind?
like the wolves in your stomach
look at my throat
a swollen and tender wisp
harrower of the earth

♦ ♦ ♦

Now how I came to be?
ahhhhhhh
ogii-kinoosidoon 'i aadizookaan gaa-tibaadodang[50]
I who have shaken around the world
around the moon
where it is very cold
around the sun
where it is very hot
through the light sings
and I sing to them
we sing together
you see everything is round
all is a circle
that is the way of the world

I was a man, once, Anishnabe
like you, now I am like these bones
you see scattered around your palisade
a long time ago I lived as the Anishnabeg
lived with my people, my family
we were happy then, before the coming
of the biiwide[51]

I had a younger brother
his name was Waub-oozoo[52]
we went everywhere together
hunting, fishing and went along to war
my little brother loved me so much
he was respected in our village as a great hunter
he ran down a deer
for a whole day once
the manitous had pity on him
even in the harshest weather
he could get something

One day a woman came to our village
her name was Beewun[53]
she was beautiful, and she fell
in love with my brother
she cooked his meat for him
kept him warm and pleased at night
they fell in love
and I was envious of him
I asked myself how could I feel this way
after all he is my brother and I should be happy
for him

I found myself staring at Beewun
wishing she would touch me like she
did my brother, I knew these feelings
were not custom, but I could not help myself
my soul longed for Beewun's touch
her laughter made my heart yearn even more
more than I could bear
the way she looked at Waub-oozoo
made my heart wretch

I could no longer bare it
I told them I was leaving for awhile
my brother asked
why would I leave?
there was plenty of game
our enemies were far away
there were many young single women
in the village and I was a good provider
but I only had room in my heart for Beewun
my brother's own wife!

I thought up an excuse
because what he said was true
our enemies were far away
and there was plenty of game
and many single women in our village

there was no reason for me to leave
I lied
I said I had a longing to wonder for awhile
to see the country
I thought this would kill the pain in my heart
the craving I had for Beewun
I thought this when I was a man
my heart was filled with a dilemma
a lust for my brother's wife and the
Anishnabeg way of respect for others and oneself
with both sadness and a wickedness in my heart
I left

I began to paddle my canoe
my head full of confusion
I sought to wonder away from those
I loved
I thought this would rid me of my strong feelings
for Beewun
I paddled all day
and into the evening
when I camped
I was still restless for Beewun
beneath my covers I could not sleep
all I could see was Beewun
her long flowing hair, her eyes staring

craving me, her body
softly touching me
I could not sleep
I lit a torch to guide my canoe
and began to paddle again
I paddled for days
until near exhaustion
I could finally paddle no more
and fell nearly dead
on the furthest shores from my home
and from Beewun

Some Indians found me there
they spoke a similar language to mine
languishing on the shore
around me they gathered
their voices sounded distant
they carried me to their village
to let the elders decide what to do with me
there they fed me meat and let me rest until
I was well enough to stand
to meet the old men of the village
there around the fire we spoke little
they wondered if I was lost
why I had come to them
a stranger

it was a polite way to ask
how they had found me on their shores
because Indians are not nosy

I told them I was a traveller
I had wondered far from
my village to see the country
"Was there no game in your country?"
one asked
"There was"
I replied
they shook their heads
smoked and left it at that
that was the way Indians were long ago

I stayed for a couple of days
and when I was rested enough
I went with the men of the village
on a hunting party
and on that day
I shot two deer and the men were envious
I shared the meat with the people
the next day I went on another hunting party
and being out of arrows
I ran a deer down and killed it
this too I brought back and shared with the people

this time instead of being envious
the men were more hospitable saying
"He is not just lucky, he is a good hunter
perhaps he should stay"

I knew that I should have left right there
but I stayed until the green leaves turned to brown
and until even the snow came and piled deep
I did not leave
in those days when I was yet a man
my heart grew fond of my new friends
to listen and see their children play
as all children do, to go on the hunt
and even raiding parties
against their enemies
my heart became very tender toward them
to listen to the wisdom of the old men
late into the darkness of the night
and even the sacred winter stories
aadizookaan[54]

Even then, the laughter of the children
the wisdom of the old men
could not quell the thunder I felt in
my heart for Beewun
her soft skin

her laughter
her shuddering touch
the way she looked
always haunting me
always wanting to return home

I went to my friends
and told them I was intending
to return home
after the sap was boiled into syrup
and they pleaded for me to stay
take myself a wife
there were many good women in that village
I told them my heart was longing to return home
and they finally relented to let me leave
with good account
and heavy hearts
so in the spring I took my canoe
and began the long journey
back to my village
little did I know that
fate would turn my longing
back into envy
and envy always becomes hatred

After many days of travel I returned to my village
my parents were there to greet me as was
my brother Waub-oozoo
the object of my envy and his wife Beewun
the object of my desire
I told of my travels and the people I'd met
and soon things were like I'd never left
I wanted Beewun and that was that
I devised a plan to kill my brother
and have Beewun for myself
I intended to drown him

One day
I asked my brother to come fishing with me
he agreed and I paddled
to the far end of a lake near where a river ran
and the water was fast
there in the canoe I grabbed him
my own brother
and threw him into the water
I watched him go down
screaming for me to help him
I only watched
my heart was completely wicked
my brother disappeared under the water
I looked around to see if anybody had

witnessed what I had done
there was only a lone bird high
in the pines, it flew away
disgusted at what it had seen

I paddled back to the village and told them
that Waub-oozoo had fallen into the rapids
and drowned
my parents and Beewun began to cry and wail
the whole village was sad because my brother was
well loved
I destroyed that
now I am here aki[55]
of neither the living or the dead

You see after that day
Beewun lost all her womanly charms
although I tried, her affection had disappeared
with my brother beneath the water
she was found dead one day, drowned
and everyone said she died of a broken heart
I destroyed it
and I could no longer live
sleep became nothing but
nightmares
the days ran together

meaningless
with that I paddled
my canoe to the middle of a lake
and threw myself in
sinking I could see the land of the dead
where everything tastes like ash
but is the same as it is here
there I could not go
I could not be dead
I could not live alive
"He killed his brother"
they said
"He lusted after his brother's wife"
they said
this the dead said
the dead said this

I would not enter the aki
of my kinfolk
of the ones I love
my bones rattle across the earth
across the moon
dancing, rattling
indishkweshim[56]
of the circle that is all life
that great hoop until it is broken

it is my bones
you hear in the medicine
dances of the Indians
I answer
I fly high above the world
near the sun where it is
very hot
near the moon where it is
very cold
I fly to the end
where men cannot go
where they cannot live
because I am both
alive and dead
at the same time

This is my story Zhaaganaash
I name this land
I was once a man like you Zhaaganaash
until the wolves in my belly overtook me

♦ ♦ ♦

Jiibayaabooz opened his eyes
the grandfathers and grandmothers were gone
what his vision meant, he did not know
he made his way out of his madoodison[57]
and into a cold running stream nearby
to refresh himself
he collected some cedar and thanked the tree
of the west
to boil tea to sustain his body
and regain his strength
after a long and enduring sweat
drinking it
he sat in the high snow
inendaagwad[58]
he remembered how he got to this place
all the time travelling
looking for his adversary
the Great North Wind
he'd come to this place to find and to slaughter

It was a long time before
the earth was torn, before the
wavers of the stick, Wemitigoozh
and those who fell from the sky, Zhaaganaash

clattered on Turtle's back
stumbling through aski
looking for zhooniyaa[59]
what noise did they make?
clamouring for the wolves in their bellies
these he did not understand, at all

He thought again
about his village long ago
before this time
his brother Maudjee-kawiss
a great hunter and warrior
he had killed many brave
from Moningwunakuaning[60]
to Lenapehoking
for the protection and to fulfill prophecy
the flight of the Anishnabeg
in the west, he laid low many
in the east, he fought many Windigos[61]

In that time there was a village
with many Windigos
who were terrorizing the Anishnabeg that lived there
the Windigos would come every morning
and grab two or three Indians
tear them limb from limb

feast, drink their blood, even sucking the marrow
from their bones
these Windigos were ferocious in their hunger
with every Indian they devoured
they swelled up until they were taller than
the trees in that country
brutish, without lips, their jagged teeth
a scowling, screeching madness
their shrieking could be heard all across that country

The chief of that village
was helpless against them
all of the brave me had fallen
their bodies and guts were consumed by those
raving Windigos
the people were withering away
like snow before the summer sun
there was none left to raise a war against them
all was lost

The old men of the village took out their hand drums
and began to call on the spirit world
because this is what is done
when men have done all they could do
the women began to sing and smudge with sage
that sacred women's medicine
calling on the spirit world
that world that shakes our world from time to time

The Windigos heard the singing
and began to tremble
the head Windigo, their chief
said to the Indians
"Why don't you stop that noise
no one can hear you
it bothers our rest
why don't you just accept your fate
all your brave men are gone
we have devoured them
crushed their bones with our jaws
and their blood we drank and yet
we are not full"

But the Indians would not stop singing or drumming
for this power was what their ancestors gave to them
Maudjee-kawiss was way to the west
tracking a bear he wanted to kill and eat
when he heard the singing and drumming of the people
he stopped in his trailing of the bear
and began to make his way to the sound
the bear was glad at his turn of fortune
for he too knew Maudjee-kawiss was a
great hunter and mighty warrior

Maudjee-kawiss made his way
crossing from the other side of gichigami[62]
that sea that used to be a mountain
he stepped over the Apalwahči mountains
and saw the Windigos
and when they saw Maudjee-kawiss
they went into a shrill and all the
trees in that country
trembled with fear

The chief Windigo spoke
"How dare you come to disturb our feast
now you will become part of it
a great warrior like you Maudjee-kawiss
makes me want to smack my lips if I had any
why would you bother with these small lowly Indians?"

Maudjee-kawiss did not speak
but swung his heavy war club
splitting the chief Windigo's head in two
he drove his club into the horrible face of another
the Indians around there began to cut
the Windigos' heads off with their stone knives
to keep them dead

The other Windigos
upon seeing their head man butchered
ran into the forest
Maudjee-kawiss went after them
slew them like a ravenous wolf
kills a den of coyote pups
when it finds them
so great was the carnage in that country

The Indians there rejoiced and cut off all the
heads of the Windigos
threw their icy hearts into a great fire they had made
for this way the ferocious Windigos cannot come back
to harrow the living

After Maudjee-kawiss had destroyed
all the Windigos in that place
he feasted with the Indians there
and saw that there were many beautiful widows
he decided he would take one for a wife
and the old men welcomed the union
and were glad to call Maudjee-kawiss
nimishoomis[63]

After many days of feasting
Maudjee-kawiss went out hunting and
brought back many moozoo
and that other one waawaashkeshi
for the women and old men of the village
enough to last them through the winter
because he loved them
then Maudjee-kawiss took his new wife
back to his village
to meet his parents Aepunggishimook and Winonah
his brothers
Nanaboozoo, Jiibayaabooz and Pukawiss
Maudjee-kawiss took his wife up to Manidoowaazh[64]
where the land was begun again
after the flood
near Baawitigong[65]
when the clans gathered there
the place where the Wemitigoozhi put up a cross
as a claimcccoola
and the Indians tore it down
in those days the people gathered
to trade, tell stories and fish
the young people would become sweethearts
and express their affection for each other
it was nearing dagwaagin[66]

when the Indians would harvest the Manoomin[67]
all were happy then
that was long time ago
there were many more Indians then
than there are now
before the rotting faces begun

Maudjee-kawiss was proud to show his beautiful wife
to his family and tell of the things he'd done
he began to gloat
especially to Jiibayaabooz
he liked to tease the most
because Jiibayaabooz was the smallest and the youngest
of the brothers
"Look Jiibayaabooz
I have gotten myself
a young and beautiful wife
eh-hey! see my war club!
I have put away many a Windigo with it
they shook with fear and cried for pity
before I slaughtered them
you see Jiibayaabooz
you could not do these things
you are too small and puny
to face even the feeblest Windigo"

At this Jiibayaabooz took great offence
to be taunted like this in front of his entire family
Jiibayaabooz replied to his older brother
"I am not afraid, the manitous have gifted me
with songs and chants and poetry
I am not afraid
I will kill the greatest of the Windigo tribe
I will kill Beboonikae[68]"

With this Jiibayaabooz gathered
his axe, bows, and arrows
to take with him
to travel north to find his adversary
Nanaboozoo and Pukawiss
told him not to go
that Beboonikae was too great an adversary
for any of them
but it was too late
his pride had spoken and words cannot be taken back

Jiibayaabooz set out
his mother, Winonah, watched him go
with a sadness in her heart
he travelled far from Manidoowaazh
to a place called Wabishkkegin[69]
he remembered

that is how he found himself in this place
the very edge of the land of the Anishnabeg
he pushed on, turning east
he went into the land of the Amikwaa[70]
near that place where
Nanaboozoo chased a giant beaver
and then on through the land
of the *big river people*
he moved on further and further
resting at a place called kachibadjiwan[71]

He stopped there for awhile
asking the Indians if they'd seen Beboonikae
they said they'd had and that she had taken
a great many of their number
they told him that when she came it was with
great fury
great madness
kicking up the snow around her feet
that all the Indians around had heard of his
challenge to Beboonikae
she howled incessantly over their lodges
their medicine men decided
to have a ceremony
to bring calm back to their land

Jiibayaabooz listened
as they told their story
Beboonikae made her way
down from the north
as she stepped through the land
she caused the trees to shiver and their leaves to fall
her breathing made the lakes turn to ice
that the Indians were no longer able to fish
even the black bears that roamed the country
hid at the sound of her coming

Moozoo disappeared
and could not be found anywhere
the beavers stayed in their lodges
even the thunder birds left their high abode
flew south
all the animals disappeared
frightened at the sight
and the sound of Beboonikae coming
even the days disappeared unable to bear
the sound of that thunder from her throat
then she appeared in their camp
dressed in her whitest winds
she shrieked when she spoke
the children cried when she did
all the Indians huddled in their lodges

none would go out to meet her
except for one old man, Goshkongesi[72]
he told her that she should leave
"Go back to where you came from
you have scared all the game away
and we are unable to endure
our people have nothing to eat
since you've come to our land
even the birds have fled far away"

This angered Beboonikae and she replied to him
"You are but a little thing to me Goshkongesi
not even a fart
I have travelled far
I have come now
but where are my sisters?
Niibin[73], Ziigwan[74], Dagwaagin[75]
they have fled
I am the earth now
even Mishipeshu[76] is hidden in his lair
my white shroud covers the world
there is nothing you can do but hide
Goshkongesi, hide beneath the snow
like all the others!"

Goshkongesi would not relent
he challenged Beboonikae to a game of skill
if he won, Beboonikae would call her she sisters back
if he lost, he'd leave his family
which was most dear to him and
stay with her all the rest of the winter
that was the wager

"I do not need to play your game of skill
little Anishnabe
you cannot change it
this is the way it is
nishiime[77]
you must be out of your mind
to believe it can be changed
even if one of my sisters came
the world would be upside down
the world would be without shape
there would be great confusion
who would tell the sap to run
who would tell the flyers of the earth to leave and
come back
when the Anishnabeg would not know when leave
and return to their fishing places
yes it is a time for the earth to rest
all rest

the bear rest
the skunk rest
the soil rest
all rest"

With that Goshkongesi got himself on a high tree stump
facing south
he began calling to Ziigwan
because after all
he was a little bit crazy
and with this Beboonikae
swept him beneath her shawl of snow
changing him into a bird
a way in the woods
calling the warm weather
for the Anishnabeg
he would not leave behind
since that night we have fasted
and dreamed many days
the thunder beings returning
the trees budding
our niinimoshenh, Makwa waking
but none of this has come to pass

Upon hearing the peoples' plight
Jiibayaabooz took some skin
from the baapaagimaak[78]
and some deer hide making a hand drum
he gave it to the people and told them
that that next time they see Goshkongesi
to give him the drum that he could call Ziigwan
back to the people
until that time
Jiibayaabooz breathed into the nearby river
and pleaded for the fish there to sustain
the Anishnabeg at the moment
and only the sucker fish answered
only the sucker fish had pity on them
Jiibayaabooz sang and gave asemaa to the fish
for its thoughtfulness
these people were grateful and in honour to the fish
became Namebinug[79]
and were renowned for their wisdom and knowledge
that time of year was called namebini-giizis
that the people would always remember

Jiibayaabooz left that village
he went to another place
where there lived
a giant serpent that antagonized the land

all around there
the Anishnabeg there could not
go out and hunt because of it
when Jiibayaabooz met them
they told him of their plight
that they could not go out and hunt
to get food for their families
for fear of the giant snake
that had slithered out of the mountains
further north some time ago

Jiibayaabooz listened to their story
seeing their withered flesh
he had pity on them
he became angry at this snake and the
trouble it had caused the people
he promised he would kill the snake
the Anishnabeg there said
the snake was resting in a deep ravine
near a small creek not too far from their village
they called the snake Mishi-ginebig

Jiibayaabooz waited until night fell
and then crept into the ravine
where Mishi-ginebig was resting
Jiibayaabooz could see its great horns standing up

for the snake it was very big and very powerful
Jiibayaabooz took out his bow
and released one of his arrows into the beast
with this Mishi-ginebig let out a loud scream
rearing its huge frightful head and
saw that it was Jiibayaabooz

"Ah it is only the little brother
I was awoken with fear that
it might be your older brother, Maudjee-kawiss
who is fearless and killed many in the east and the west
there is no warrior greater
or even that trembling tail, Nanaboozoo[80]
whose cunning and trickery
always seem to give him good luck
or even Pukawiss, the disowned one
because his father saw no value in his dancing
or dressing in his fine clothes or his love of life
but it is only the little one
that dreams and chants
what can you do, dream me away?
sing me out of this fine place?
with so many Anishnabeg to sustain me
I love it here in my comfortable place"

Mishi-ginebig let it be known that he was not
frightened in the least of Jiibayaabooz
Mishi-ginebig lunged at Jiibayaabooz
but he jumped back and then quickly
leaned forward and cut off one of
Mishi-ginebig's horns with his axe
at this the great snake was in shock
and began again to speak
"Nishiime! Where did you get such ferocity?
that is not like you
Sing! See if you can lull me to sleep, have pity"

Infuriated Jiibayaabooz swung again
this time slashing through
the great snake's thick skin
Mishi-ginebig shaken took off up the creek bed
following it north
thrashing and twisting about in great pain
widening the creek until it became a mighty river
when the snake got to the head waters
he leaped and dove into a high cliff
Jiibayaabooz chased him but could not get into the cliff
Mishi-ginebig stayed in the mountains for fear of his life

Later the Anishnabeg came out of their lodges
to see what was done and said
"Gii-nameshin a'aw ginebig o'omaa gii-pimi-ayaagwen"[81]
it was on that high cliff they built a madoodiswan[82]
that Mishi-ginebig might assist them in their bawaajigan[83]
and that they would remember what Jiibayaabooz
was able to do for them
they said that
great serpent still hides there
beneath the rock

♦ ♦ ♦

Jiibayaabooz found himself in the north of the country
he knew Beboonikae was close
he could hear her
the howling was incessant
calling to him
come cousin
I have been searching for you
I have even sent out Bakaak to find you
that sad and forever lonely
flying bag of bones, but he has only found
the carriers of the stick and the
ones who seemed to fall from the sky
and yet he has not returned but damned to fly

around the world until
the last hoop
of earth is broken

Poor Bakaak, no one has pity
where are you my niinimoshenh?[84]
I have been searching for you
calling many months
since I've heard you've come to kill me
my young puny Jiibayaabooz
what would put such foolishness in your heart?
I've have been on the earth much longer than you
I was greater than I am now, vast
I had mercy on my sisters
that was when we decided to divide this island
into four as a share for each
we pitied the poor Anishnabeg then
even now I am greater than you
Jiibayaabooz and this foolish thing
you have brought to us
only because of your brother
Maudjee-kawiss
and your foolish pride
I give the world rest, that needed sleep
that is the only way one can dream my Jiibayaabooz
my lovely gagiibaadizi[85]

here I am, my frozen shroud covering the world
show yourself to me Jiibayaabooz
show yourself to me
show yourself to me gagiibaadizi
that we may put an end to this thing

Jiibayaabooz followed her voice
he found that his feet began to grow
into thin and strong shoes
that made walking above the snow
clean and quiet
higher and higher above the snow
he grew
coming closer and closer to his foe

He called out to Beboonikae
through the numbing blizzard
I am here Beboonikae, I have travelled a long time
to come to you, tarried through your deepest snows
seen the hardship you bring *the original people*
cause the game to be put out of sight
even the mighty thunder birds cannot bare
and must journey to the zhaawanong[86]
the world is made silent and deep
with you here, even fish are
not easy to have

The original people have always given you
respect and honour
and still you treat them with such contempt
I am getting close to you Beboonikae
I have brought my axe
my drum
and my most exceeding mettle
because I love them

With this Jiibayaabooz
leaped on to Beboonikae
hitting her with his axe
he only split the wind and Beboonikae
rose up again, blinding him in a blizzard
throwing him onto the ground
while Jiibayaabooz lay there
Beboonikae spoke
"You are no match to me little one
although your heart is immense
your body betrays it"

Jiibayaabooz struggled to lift his body
as it froze to the snow
"Beboonikae! you have brought that terrible ever
ravenous beast, Windigo, here
to terrorize and destroy the people

whose heart is made
of the coldest ice and jagged teeth gnaw the bones
of this, our cousins, and all the land
that lanky thing
my brother, Mishi-ginebig, has
destroyed many
yet they grow taller than the trees
and become plentiful
and robust in their greed
I will put an end to it"

Beboonikae gave him another cold blast
and Jiibayaabooz fell fused to the frozen ground
slowly he began to freeze to death
his heart slower and slower
beating out his death song
knowing he was dying
in the cause of the good
of the people
he began to pass into the land of the dead
he came again up from beneath the snow
leaving behind his hand drum
he gifted that power to the Anishnabeg
that they could call the ancestors that power
that can tremble the world
there he drifted to that place

of the ancestors to call on the spirit world
because this is what is done
when men have done all they could
that world that touches this one
that world that shakes our world from time to time
that time cannot measure
those that are called with
Jiibayaabooz's hand drum
for *the original people*

1. Rabbit spirit
2. Shaking Tent ceremony
3. Snapping Turtle spirit
4. "Ojibwa Indians" or literally "The original people"
5. Anishnabeg for "Moose"
6. Thank you, thank you very much
7. Moose spirit
8. Mi'kmaq for "Windigo"
9. Quebec Cree for "Windigo"
10. Anishnabeg for "flying skeleton"or "bones coved in skin"
11. Anishnabeg for "Thunderbird" or "Thunderer"
12. Horned serpent
13. Wolf, brother to Nanboozhoo
14. Reservations
15. Variola major, small pox
16. February, literally "Sucker fish moon"
17. French for "Werewolf"
18. Anishnabeg for "Frenchman"
19. French for "me"
20. Attributed to Jacques Cartier upon arriving in North America
21. Mishipeshu, underwater lynx
22. Cowry Shell
23. Deer
24. French for "mercy"
25. "Dwellers of the Peninsula"
26. Abnakis
27. Underwater lynx
28. Odawa for "the Sioux"
29. Ottawa river
30. Bear
31. Wolf
32. Tobacco
33. Anishnabeg woman
34. Anishnabeg for "I am"
35. Anishnabeg for "I am from"
36. Anishnabeg for "east"
37. Anishnabeg for "Englishman"
38. "You can hear my grandmother across the lake?"
39. An Indian tribe that inhabited Delaware and New York
40. Great spirit
41. Appalachian mountains
42. Lenape for "town"
43. Iroquois village near present-day Quebec City
44. Anishnabeg for "boat or canoe"

45. Played lacrosse
46. 17th century French
47. Anishnabeg for "money"
48. His grandfather
49. Crowfoot, Blackfoot, warrior and orator 1830 - 1890
50. "That is an old story" or literally "He made the legend he told long"
51. Stranger
52. "The Rabbit" or "One with a White Tail"
53. A woman's name, down or fur
54. A legend, myth
55. Earth, land, soil
56. Dances at the end
57. Sweatlodge
58. To think about his destiny
59. "Money" from the French "jaune" (yellow), the colour of gold
60. La Pointe, Wisconsin, "The seventh stopping place"
61. The spirit of selfishness, perhaps from Anishnabeg "weenin n d'd'igooh"
62. Lake Superior
63. Grandfather
64. Manitouwadge, literally "Cave of the Great Spirit"
65. Sault Ste. Marie, literally "Place of the rapids"
66. Autumn
67. Wild rice
68. Winter maker
69. "The sheet is white"
70. Anishnabeg for "Beaver People" or "Descendant of"
71. Underground river
72. Ruffled grouse
73. Summer
74. Spring
75. Autumn
76. The underwater lynx
77. Younger brother
78. Black ash tree
79. Sucker fish clan
80. "Shaking" or "trembling tail"
81. The trail of the snake shows it must have passed by here
82. Sweatlodge
83. A dream, a vision
84. "Male cousin," here it is used as "sweetheart"
85. Foolish or silly
86. South